# Venom To Victory

By Dr. Elle Moore

Publishing by KDP Publishing

Copyright ©BlkPenPublishing

ISBN: 9798730940802

@BlkPenPublishing

# Foreword

John 8:32, "Then you will know the truth, and the truth will make you free" (NIV).

A door can be an instrument in which to entrap you or which to liberate you. This awe-inspiring writing will do the latter. The "truth" of relationship work is embedded on each page. What a privilege we have to "swing" free from a long list of emotional and mental bondages that have been stored in the archives of our souls.

Dr. Elle Moore shares, with complete transparency, her heart and her experiences from many angles that will meet each reader where they are.

Through her formal education in the field of psychology, her experience as a licensed minister, and life lessons, she brings a perspective and insight that is revolutionary, enlightening, and life giving. Each page will cause you to breathe again as you identify yourself, commit to doing the work of healing, and beginning again

~ Lisa Scott

# **<u>Dedication</u>**

I wrote this for you. The venom that tried to kill you will ultimately be your launching pad of victory. For this reason, I believe in your worth. You are valuable. You are worthy of true, genuine, authentic love.

Transcend your emotional valley.
Ascend in liberty of your uniqueness.
You are an amazing & unique visionary.
Disown exhaustion.
Amplify your strength.
Starve fear.
Never settle.
That voice in your head that keeps you alive; amplify it to a crescendo.
Be the super hero you were created to be.

This contextual journey of self-love transitions from venom to victory to help you pilot your relationships, find your strength, and live your worth. You can identify, remove, and transcend hurt or disappointment as you voyage through your personal and professional relationships.

Be encouraged, motivated, healed, and strengthened.

You are valuable. You are powerful. You <u>will</u> live to the fullest capacity of your being. You <u>will</u> be encouraged. You <u>will</u> identify new solutions. Not only will you survive; you <u>will</u> unapologetically advance, stronger, along your journey. You <u>will</u> be okay. You <u>will</u> be okay. You <u>will</u> be okay.

# **<u>Acknowledgments</u>**

My relationships and numerous individuals that have invested in my leadership maturity and experience.

# Table of Contents

## THE RELATIONSHIPS

## THE RECOVERY

## THE RELIGION

# **Opening Prayer**

God, help the person reading this to search the areas of their heart that need healing and resolution.

Invade the cracks and trenches of brokenness. Like a soothing aloe: heal, revive, restore, mend, and reconstruct them to wholeness.

Make the dry bones live.

Resurrect a lively stone and ignite confidence and peace in living the fullest of their "being". The "being" that You created them to be: the wonderful, person of purpose ... Amen.

# **Preface**

This journey will require you to be true to yourself. The real you, that God created you to be. Do not be afraid of being exactly who you are. This means that you will make mistakes. You will forget. You will remember. You will say the wrong thing at times and even change dramatically throughout your growth. Guess what? It is all okay. The mistakes you make (venom) are prerequisites of the (victory) that is to come. Your venom and your victory are both part of your journey of unapologetic strength.

# THE

# RELATIONSHIPS

# 1

# EMPTY CUP

I've esteemed your worth higher than my own
Giving rays of energy to unrequited affirmation
Counterfeit the truest love left me empty
I'm Empty…
I am empty. I gave to you until I had nothing. I
invested my all, thinking it was the "right" thing to
do. All I want is for you to Refill me. Restore me.
Refill me… Restore...


Fill my cup with the faintness of your fingertips
Pour in lyrics of desire and passion
Topped off with exploratory horizons of new earth
beneath my feet
Overflow me with your embrace

Rarely do we recognize the signs of emotional and spiritual depletion until we are empty.

We give and give because we have love for others that goes beyond recognition.
We give to see others succeed.
We give to invest in love.
We give to show them that we care.

Who will invest in your dreams?
Who will adore your flaws?
Who will laugh with you to peace?
Who will embrace your cleverest smile?

People, good people, are coming to pour into you. While they're on their way, God is showing you how to pour restoration into yourself. You won't remain empty for long.

# 2

# STANDARDS

"Once a month"? Um, what about the other 29 days? Would I receive a phone call or text message? Do you even care to make me a part of your life? Was I not a priority?

I dated a guy who talked about spending time with me but only told me about his experiences after everything already occurred. I was never a part *of* his life experiences.
He would go see a movie. Instead of taking me with him to the movie theatre, he went by himself and told me all the details afterward.

I had to remove myself from that relationship and reserve my heart for someone that wanted to make me a part *of* their life and not add me as a responsibility to the end of their day. That was my standard and it was set.

See, if they want to see you, they'll find a way. If not, they'll make an excuse. Everyone gets the same 24 hours. People make time for the things they want. Even if they're busy, they always have the option to take you with them and include you in the errands of their day.

You don't have to accept someone who does not love you the way you deserve to be loved.
You deserve someone who wants to call you. You deserve someone who wants to see you. You deserve someone who will include you in the busyness of their life.

You are not asking too much.
The right person will call.

The right person will make plans and show you that they care for you.

The right person will give you a healthy amount of attention where you can maintain your independence and still grow together.

The person God has for you will be more than happy to show you how much they appreciate you being in their life.

They will value your presence so much that you'll forget the losers that wasted your time.

They will be obsessed with getting to know you.

God has created you as the missing piece of their puzzle. This means that God has created them to know exactly how to love you, already in divine design. They are already created to indulge you with the perfect amount of attention, desire, and time apart. When the two of you meet, you'll know it.

# **<u>PRAYER</u>**

God, expose any standards we've set that are not
inspired by You.

Guide our standards toward healthy relationships of
improvement.

Govern our commitments to love others the way You
love us: continuously.

Grant us Your wisdom, knowing that divine insight
helps develop our relationships and our "love
standards".

"Set your standard and keep it set."

"Run for your life or stay here and die"

# 3

## <u>EMOTIONAL ABUSE</u>

I was physically and emotionally abused the majority of my childhood, feeling bound and trapped with no way of escape. Having to revisit the presence of my oppressors over and over again reopened wounds of pain, helplessness, and lack of trust. The physical abuse shaped my desire to trust others, but I lacked the ability to trust because of wounds and bruises of vulnerability.

Once I completed the process of mental and emotional healing in forgiving my abusers, there was no way in hell that I would allow myself to suffer physical or emotional abuse as an adult.

Some say that emotional abuse is far more damaging than physical abuse. The roller coaster of up and down is draining and meant to kill your mental health.

I remember 9 months into our relationship when he started yelling and screaming at the top of his lungs. He screamed himself out the door. His next words included an apology with flowers and a dinner invitation.

I remember him yelling at the top of his lungs and then apologizing; telling me how he loved me; then yelling at me all over again. When I asked him about the unresolved issue, he "hulked".

I remember the moment like it was last week.

I remember the "out-of-body experience".
I remember seeing myself standing completely still in the center of the room.

He was yelling at the top of his lungs, pointing his finger in my face, then up in arms. He stomped in and out of the room slamming doors and throwing whatever he could find that wouldn't break. I could see us both, but couldn't hear anything he was saying. Everything was completely silent. At that moment, the voice of God spoke to me clearly and said,

"Run for your life or stay here and die."

God reminded me of the damage and death that results from lingering and staying in relationships too long. The scripture reference given was Genesis 19:16 that reads, "But he (Lot) hesitated. So the men seized his hand and the hand of his wife and the hands of his two daughters, for the compassion of the LORD was upon him; and they brought him out, and put him outside the city".

See, God loves you, and loved me enough to snatch me out of that emotionally abusive relationship. That was the day that I left and tried my best not to look back.

Empty threats like, "you don't have a place to go", "you don't have anyone else to love you, or you don't have any money", are confirmations that it is beyond time for you to leave. When your life is in jeopardy, you are not thinking about calling a moving truck and scheduling a pick up in the next 4-5 days. No beloved, you grab what you can carry and you run! Don't worry about where you will live, or the financial responsibility. Your life is far more valuable than these.

In losing them, you gain your peace.

God and your freedom want you to detach from everything that is killing your spirit. It may not necessarily be physical abuse but it is draining your energy. God has told you to end it multiple times before. God has already made a way of escape for you. You are responsible for your choice to be free. You just need to move. Your life will begin again when you ignite your strength and courage to walk away.

# 4

## **MOVING MOTIVATION**

You are strong.

You deserve to live free of physical and emotional abuse.

You deserve to be loved, truly loved, and respected.

You are not a punching bag.

Your heart is not a piñata.

Decide that your life is worth more by walking away from the hurt, mental anguish, and pain. You deserve healing. You deserve restoration. You deserve peace.

# **PRAYER**

God, give us strength to break the chains of emotional and physical abuse.

Reveal the intentions of those that we call "friends" to expose unhealthy relationships that are spiritually detrimental.

Apprehend fear that keeps us bound and trapped in complacency.

Create liberties above the mental jail of distress.

Embrace us with people that will protect, cover, and assist us in securing shelter, healing, and support.

# 5

## <u>BLINK & GONE</u>

He said all the right things in the beginning. Then his enthusiasm turned into lack of planning and last minute excuses. "I'm sad that I can't give you the world," he said, as an excuse for his disinterest.

Sir, I never asked for the world. I only asked for the same amount of love and affection that captured my heart in the beginning of our relationship.

Where is that? Are you comfortable now? You've settled? Really, after only 30 days?
He said, "we don't have to talk every week, or see each other every month."

Really? You live 10 minutes away. How did you go from calling me multiple times a day and seeing me quite a few times within your week to, "we don't have to talk"?

Sigh…
In these moments of confrontation you either:
Lose your standard by accepting their new lack of effort or
Keep your standard and risk ending the relationship.

Some people will try to make you feel guilty for requesting simple things like spending time or making an effort. Those two are necessary in any relationship.

You are not asking for too much.
Your requests are not unreasonable.
You are not insecure.
You are not high maintenance.

You are expecting genuine love from the wrong person.

Why should you even have to ask?

Your love-mate will make an effort and want to spend time with you. They will want to show you that you are an important priority. They will tell you they love you in their touch and with their words. Your love-mate will love you longer than 1 week, 90 days or 6 months. Your love-mate will make an effort to show you consistency and longevity.

Love is patient, love is kind. It does not envy, it does not boast, it is not proud. It does not dishonor others, it is not self-seeking, it is not easily angered, it keeps no record of wrongs. Love does not delight in evil, but rejoices with the truth. It always protects, always trusts, always hopes, always perseveres (1st Cor 13).

Be committed to love regardless of outside distractions or complacency. Make an effort to show love with consistency and longevity.

Love like you have never been hurt.

This includes you, loving you.

So, never fear losing someone whose behavior doesn't make you feel loved. Seriously, if they are not treating you right, then there really is no loss, anyway.

Furthermore, their behavior is not your fault. Meaning, you didn't do anything wrong to make them treat you this way. Don't blame yourself. Don't you dare feel guilty for having love standards. Yes, you have a big heart and it has endured the blow of another ended relationship. It's not the end. Your story is a continuous journey. LOVE is a comma, not a period.

# 6

# <u>ESCAPE THE LIES</u>

He lied about taking care of some business. Later, he told me that he lied. I asked him why he felt the need to lie to me. He responded by focusing on the fact that he "came clean" and was truthful, eventually.

Even after forgiving him, what remained was the root cause for the reason he decided to lie, initially. I asked him if we could talk about the reason "why" he lied, to try and identify the root. He avoided the discussion. See, he never wanted to deal with or address the reason he chose to lie. He didn't want us to expose the root.

Was it fear?
Was it embarrassment?
Was he no longer able to maintain appearances?

Was his mask getting too heavy?

Still, he kept saying, "but eventually, I told you the truth".

Well, guess what? If they can't identify or address the reason why they lied initially, then it is safe to say that they will probably lie again. Maybe, not right away. But indeed it will happen.

I forgave him and reminded him of my standard against lying. I also realized that no one is perfect and we all make mistakes. So, wearing "grace goggles", I continued with the relationship. At that time, "1" lie was not enough for me to walk away from the man that I loved.

Then a few days later, in conversation, he mentioned not being honest regarding an important matter. I asked myself, was this a lie, per say? We are all entitled to change our minds, right? Of course. So, I told him how important he was to me, that I desired to understand how he feels, and that we should always be able to tell each other what's going on in our heads. So, I continued the relationship with "grace goggles". The following week, he tells me in mid-conversation that he was keeping secrets from me for months. Wait, what? Yes, at that point I thought, really, dude? I knew that my standard was being compromised. I knew that although I loved him, I needed to self-reflect. Did I want to be with someone who kept secrets from me, lied about their feelings or the things they've done? Doesn't respect come with honesty? Did I like the results? No, I had to choose myself. I needed to respect my feelings and my heart. He wasn't a bad person. He was actually quite kind and attractive. Still, my standard of honesty was more important than my desire to be in a relationship. Did he think I was stupid and wouldn't find out? Did I want to be with a guy who was attractive, kind, and dishonest? Did I want to be with someone who I could not trust? The answer was "No". I ended our relationship. I needed to make that decision for myself. I identified my standard and realized my self-respect required me to walk away. Leaving was not easy to do. But the alternative of staying in that relationship with someone I'll probably never be able to trust again was pointless.

It doesn't matter if the infraction is lying or infidelity. You have to set your standard.

Sure, you desire companionship.
But at what cost? Would it cost your peace of mind?
Would it cost your energy?

What is the cost to be in a relationship with someone who refuses truth in their actions?

Entertaining liars is never worth the price of a healthy heart.

The trust was gone.

The attraction diminished.

The desire to build ended.

In return, I gained confidence in valuing my worth.

In return, I gained strength in my singleness.

In return, my soul grew taller than giants.

I released the negative energy to make room for positive goodness. I gained an immediate return by investing in my worth.

"Trust" is a costly commodity.

And Baby, the price is high.

# **PRAYER**

God, please forgive us for the times that we lied to ourselves and were dishonest with others.

Help us forgive ourselves for allowing dishonest people to stay in our lives beyond their expiration.

Give us the strength to close the relationship door to liars, cheaters, and negative energy. We seal the door shut and destroy the key.

Integrity and Honesty are birthed from Respect.

Respect me first, then we can discuss the option of

romance.

# 7

## **<u>GRACE GOGGLES</u>**

Don't let "grace goggles" blind you to foolishness.

# 8

# <u>REJECTION</u>

"You see the pain as rejection. But, I am trying to protect you."

He looked incredible: tall, dark, and handsome. He was educated and charming. His scent of strong steel, flannel, and sweet cake enticed my senses. His smile ignited a room. His embrace melted me into his muscles like butter on warm toast. His chest, biceps, and shoulders were a refuge from the stress of my day. I felt secure in him. I felt confident and protected.

We were compatible spiritually, academically, and professionally.

After a few months of dating, a few concerns made me uncomfortable but for the most part, things were good. Those small concerns began to magnify into glimpses of disrespect and infidelity. I prayed first and decided to have a conversation with him about my concerns. I communicated that I wanted to work through the small things and did not think that my concerns were deal breakers. I chose to see things from his perspective and hear what he had to say. What I saw from my perspective, he could have viewed a completely different way. Right? So we talked. In response, he refused to acknowledge my feelings or concerns and made the conversation about him. He spoke about how awesome he was and that I should be appreciative that he would even talk to me because thousands of women wanted him. He then said that he didn't want to move forward or resolve any concerns.

That was the end of our conversation. I was devastated. What I thought was real turned out to be nothing to him. The spirit of rejection hit me like a ton of bricks. How did I go from being, "the perfect one for him", (his words, not mine) to just another one of his 5,000 women? It took a few moments for me to gather my emotions and pray.

I asked God why I had to endure another failed relationship. Why was expressing my feelings met with a broken heart? God's response:

"Daughter, how many times must I remind you that you deserve My best? What I have for you is better than what you think you've lost. I am protecting you from things that you don't see".
Immediately, I felt the heavy weight of rejection lifted. God was saying:

"Stop questioning what I allowed to happen. Stop replaying in your mind what you could have said or done differently. Stop thinking that you were wrong or that you asked too much of them."

The rejection you feel is a mismanagement of the emotional disconnect. You must trust that if that relationship was supposed to last, it would. Or another way to see it is, if they are meant for you, they will be back and there is nothing you can say or do to prevent it. If that relationship is meant to end, it will end; regardless of what you say or don't say. Rejection hurts, but changing your perspective to focus on God's best for you, will allow you to heal. It makes the rejection purposeful and necessary. Time will also give your heart resolve to move forward. If they cannot see how valuable you are, then they don't deserve your energy anyway.

Expensive things are often rejected by people who can't afford them.

You are only completely free from rejection and its fear when you surrender your life and experience to the sovereign God of the universe. It is okay to release the hurt and still desire companionship. A genuine companion is searching for everything you have to offer.

Remember the first rejection and hurt you thought you'd never get over? You survived, you learned, and you came out of that situation stronger and wiser because of the experience.

You were meant to have that experience to show you how strong your resolve can be, through you. Remember, your strongest moment is when you release the weight, hurt, and rejection of the experience. God knew you'd be here at this moment.

This did not take the universe by surprise. It is sovereign. God rejected them, for you, because God loves you more than you can comprehend.

God rejected them, for you, because they are not God's best for you. God has a "better love". Sure they may find someone else that better fits their wants. That is completely acceptable. When you know who you are. Rejection becomes less of a personal attack and more of an acknowledgment that 'everyone can't afford nice things'. You are so rare and valuable that people should not touch your magic with their dirty hands.

Spirit is teaching you not to settle, trust your spiritual intuition.

Only the best, for you. Only God's best for you.

# **PRAYER**

God, search our hearts for unhealed areas of rejection or disappointment.

Lord, help us find ways to heal through times of rejection, knowing that the pain is real but no match for what You can do, or must do, to strengthen our heart.

The plans You have for us are graced with Your love.

Give us rest in Your love for us; Your best for us.

Teach us to deny anything less than Your best.

We will wait on You and trust You with our heart.

Drench us with the confidence to be #GodlySpoiled

WHATEVER GOD TELLS YOU TO DO, DO IT.

(NO FEAR)

# 9

## **<u>EAGLES</u>**

Have you ever entered a room and realized that you were "above" the environment? Not in 'arrogance' or 'ego'. Just, some environments no longer honor your divine self. You've already graduated from some experiences and places.

Well guess what? You *were* "above" that space. Eagles don't fly with chickens.
You're not obligated to that environment.
Move/fly/escape/leave

Disengage from all sources of negative mediocre energy.
You're too important to "cluck" with them anymore.

You're an Eagle. #VibrateHigh #FlyHigh #Soar

Loving them does not obligate you to a corrupt relationship.

# 10

## <u>LOVE ME</u>

We are strong as individuals but stronger with one another. Embedded in our DNA is the fundamental desire to be connected to, and loved by, someone else.

In seeking that love from others, we may give away our hearts too quickly. We give love because it feels good. We only hope that the love we give will be reciprocated.

You don't have to give your love away for everyone or to everyone to get or receive love. Stop allowing other people to devalue the beauty of your love. Guard your beautiful love in every way. Ensure that you are loving yourself: healthy, mentally, physically, financially, and emotionally. Before you give your beautiful love to others, protect your love from users that want to take advantage of your pure heart.

My "self-love" changed when I realized 3 very important things:

1. Loving people unconditionally, does not guarantee or obligate them to love you in return. Furthermore, people will see your unconditional love and think that you'll be loyal to them regardless of how they treat you. They will lose respect for you and their value of you will decrease; all because you chose to love them unconditionally.

2. Only when you show love for yourself; will others love you too.

3. That "real love" you have for yourself becomes more than enough. I used to care way too much

about what people thought of me. Who cares what they think? Who cares what they say? The more you love yourself, the less you'll need the opinions/false love of others.

Progressively, intentionally, love yourself more and more every day. In this only, will you be whole.

You're Rare

# 11

## <u>ISLAND</u>

You are rare and priceless. Imagine an island that only a few wealthy, elite, people can afford the opportunity to visit.

Imagine being hidden as to protect your value from those who try to purchase you for less than you're worth.
You deserve the best, only.

Don't settle for mistreatment. Don't settle for "what they have left over". You deserve the best. You deserve the best. You deserve the best. Expect God's best, and accept God's best. You're a Rare Island.

# **<u>PRAYER</u>**

God, we trust that You know who is supposed to be in our lives and who serves no purpose.

I am grateful for opened doors and closed doors of relationships.

I commit to keeping the doors closed, that have closed, and will not grant re-entry.

I attract the right people that will build us.

I attract the right people to love us.

I attract Your best for my life.

# 13

## <u>MR. SINGLE AND SAVED</u>

Oh, this guy.

I like to call him the 'Anointed Casanova'. Dude has swag to the overflow. He's attractive, confident, spiritual, and charismatic. He pursued me really strong in the beginning. He took me on weekly dates, called multiple times within his day, and made me laugh until my stomach hurt. I noticed after a while, he began to challenge my trust because he never committed.

Even though I may not have seen it completely, my heart knew that he was "charismatic" with everyone. Females in his community all swarmed for his attention. They flirt, giggle, and are quick to brush his shoulder or hug him. They do anything to get close. He welcomed the attention as a man who enjoys the admiration of as many women as possible. Can you blame him? Absolutely not. However, if he couldn't see my worth, any attention I showed him put me in the same category as his sea of concubines. I realized he would never commit to me. He will most likely not commit to anyone. I resolved to be okay with that. He was obviously not for me, romantically. He enjoyed the endless women, the bachelor lifestyle, and the attention he received. I was just another pretty lady in the congregation of women who rave over him. I can't make him change. I don't want him to change.

More importantly, I had to examine what to accept in my life and who deserves my time.

If he thought I was worth it, he would part the Red Sea, dismiss all the other faces, and only see me.

You're worth a commitment.

You're worth not feeling like you're in competition with anyone else.

You're worth being treated like their only desire.

You must resolve within your heart that you cannot change anyone. They have to want to change for themself. Mr. Single and Saved had no reason to change. He already has everything he wants. My presence would only be joining his circus of women. I realized a committed relationship with him was not going to happen. I moved on.

No one is worth "sharing". It is okay to leave people behind. Everyone you lose is not a loss.

Fair well, good-bye, so long.
We're still friends though...
Wink*

# PRAYER

God, teach us to embrace our season of singleness. Being single is not a curse. We are satisfied. We are not lonely. We are not lacking because we are single. We have other things to do with our time. We have talents to pursue. Our prayer is that we gain the wisdom to respond quickly and directly to those who try to make us feel like we are less than valuable, because we are single.

Give us words of love for people who keep asking, "When are you going to get married?"
"When are you going to have children?"
"What happened to so-and-so"? It's annoying.

We're good, because we are complete and satisfied within ourselves.

We lack nothing. We are whole, complete. We are happy and content.

# 14

## <u>MARRIED? DO NOT PASS "GO"</u>

He was strong, charismatic, and hilarious. He was also married. Married people are not meant to entertain you.

It is extremely rude and naive of you to think that they will ever leave their spouse for you or that you two will be together. Sure, they say their marriage is unhappy. Sure they even say they want a divorce. They even say that they want to get a divorce so they can marry you. Even while going through a divorce, they are still married.

Your love is not found in anyone who is married. Even after a divorce, hearts need time to heal and lives need time to re-adjust. For some, the adjustment period after a divorce can take about two years, and you deserve that time after a divorce to determine if you even want to be in a relationship. They may want to remain single.

You don't need to give a married person time to decide.

You can avoid them all together. God's leading is never toward anyone who is already married. If they cheat on their spouse with you, they will cheat on you with someone else. The issues they have are not yours to solve. You're not responsible for fixing them. They must work through their divorce and allow God to heal them as an individual. Please leave and don't squander any more of your time. Staying will only cause you more pain and frustration. Be satisfied in your singleness until someone who is available and ready to pursue you arrives.

You deserve someone who can love you in liberty and liberally.

Relationships can be both; commitment and freedom.

# **PRAYER**

God, help us value our worth never to be someone's option or side adventure. We will no longer accept partial love. We deserve robust, full, visible, and limitless love.

*Never beg someone to love you. If they can't recognize how valuable you are in their life or how important you are to them, let them go. You've been through too much to settle for someone who doesn't choose you. You choose people that choose you. You choose you.*

# 15

## <u>PROTECTION</u>

You were supposed to protect me.

You knew my strengths, weaknesses, joys, and pain.

Instead, you expose my most sensitive pages, detailed in complete transparency, to any and everyone who would ask.

You can't protect me.

The mote, concrete walls, and alligators now surround my heart.

You violated my safety. Ripped me until I fell…. naked and bare.

You're never getting back in. Do not pass "go".

Now, I'm the one who must always protect myself.

# 16

## <u>5 LEVELS OF COMPATIBILITY</u>

1. Spiritual
2. Intellectual
3. Emotional
4. Physical
5. Financial

Get a physical pen and paper. Write down your vision, in each category, of who you want to be in your life. Then, write down who you want your partner to be. **Expect it**. Release people and things that don't align with the life you're manifesting.

# 17

## <u>STILL NOT THE ONE</u>

He was chocolate

wore suits daily

well educated

knew scripture like the back of his hand and smelled

like testosterone and brown sugar.

Things were going well.


We were compatible: academically, spiritually, and

physically.

Although he was my same height, it didn't matter.

His ambition and faith made him appear 10 feet tall.

He was it. The man of my dreams was finally here.


Womp Womp, Dead End, Narcissist, Ishmael


Still Single…

Other than him being a narcissist, I always thought we were a match.

See, we don't always understand why some relationships end. But all relationships we encounter are purposeful and contain lessons. When God closes a door, you keep it SHUT! You don't need to know everything that God is doing. You just have to trust your process and move forward.

# 18

## <u>ACCESS DENIED</u>

Your face displayed on my caller I.D. paused the beating of my heart. I forgot how beautiful you were. 7+ feet tall, dark, handsome, bald, beard, smile for days. However, I could not forget how long it took me to heal from your dagger of immaturity. I hate that you think you can come back into my life and ask for a third chance to break my heart.

Lose my number. Get off my phone. You're selfish. You don't get access to me anymore. Your grace, in my life, has expired. You don't deserve my time, you don't deserve my energy, you don't deserve my wisdom.

You had your chance to take over the world with me, exploring beaches of sand between our toes.

You had your chance to walk this path fused by our hands.

You had your chance to relish my love. Forgiving you does not grant re-entry to my life. Yes, I forgave you. More importantly, I know you are calling to apologize. You want me to help you lift your remorse.
Still, I need to protect my soul from your selfishness that only wants to toy with my HEART. You feel guilty.

You're selfish. You're only apologizing because you want me to help you lift the weighty burden of remorse you created for not valuing my worth. You're selfish.

Keep your apology.

You have to go to God for yourself, for your own healing; to lift that guilty weight.

Like I did. I had to heal on my own without you and without your apology.
Taking months to get over you.

Tears, pain, healing… I refuse to do that again. I refuse to allow you to open my heart and stab it with your dagger of destruction and deceit. You're selfish. You realized you can accomplish more with me by your side. You need my listening ear. You need my wisdom and business experience. But, I am no longer available. You decided to leave. You lost the best woman for your life. Your door is closed.

You've been blocked.

Access denied

# THE

# RECOVERY

# 19

## <u>PURPOSE & SATISFACTION</u>

You have 3 purposes in life:

1. To use your gifts, talents, and abilities to maximize your unique influence in the earth.

2. To use your gifts, talents, and abilities to help someone else become the best version of themself.

3. To live the most abundantly fulfilled life while you have breath in your lungs.

Complete satisfaction and truth only appear when your actions parallel with your purpose.

"Timeout" for dead end jobs that stress you to no end.

"Game over" for friendships that make you question your worth. Anything contrary to you maximizing your greatest purpose must be extinguished. Your satisfaction is achieved in your "Created-Purpose" only. Lovers, friends, money, will never match or fulfill you to satisfaction. You must pursue your destiny and manifest your created purpose. All our other desires become secondary accomplishments of purpose.

The universe is on your side waiting to assist you. Pursue your purpose with vigor. God is sending the provision to accomplish your goals. The right people are on their way to sow seeds of investment into your destiny. They believe in you.

Focus on being your best "human" "be"ing. Love, cherish, fight, rest, laugh, invest, give, rest, build, rest, and rest. Take time for you. When you pursue your purpose it creates opportunity for other people to walk in their purpose. The right people are waiting for you to walk in your purpose. Invest in them.

Spend time with them. Call them. Call and plan a concert, plan a dinner, plan a "do nothing" session with them. Celebrate the people who love you authentically. Celebrate the people who push you to greatness.

Your journey is so important that it MUST be celebrated. Do you recall those moments that were meant to kill you; that Venom? You were strengthened through the experience because you survived. Now you're stronger, better, and wiser. Beloved, unapologetically live in complete satisfaction, strength, and Victory.

# 20

# THE BANK OF FAITH

## Freedom From Loss and Lack

Things were growing especially difficult at work. I knew from past experiences that when things become dreadfully unreasonable at work, apply for a new position and get out! But, thank God. Instead of getting out, God was trying to strengthen me to go through. God was trying to stretch my patience. During this time, there were other lessons I needed to learn.

If you have to work with crazy people, or a jealous boss who intentionally creates obstacles for you to fail, lies or belittles you, God is trying to strengthen you or release you. God is either preparing you to stay or preparing you to leave. Be certain that change is coming.

I remember being in a place of prayer and I had no clue what God was trying to teach me. I applied for job after job and no one hired me. I applied for jobs I was qualified for, overqualified for, and under qualified for. All of the email responses I received read, "Thank you for applying… unfortunately, you were not selected for this position". I began to get discouraged. I always had a job. I worked consistently beginning at the age of 15. Even in my current position, I had no idea of the problem. My salary was exempt. I arrived to work early and stayed late. All of my performance reviews were "average" to "exceeds expectation" and my boss still despised me. I received numerous awards from my colleagues and superiors.

Still, my boss falsely accused me multiple times. Half of her 6-person team quit and she assigned me the job of her 3 former employees. She was intentionally trying to set me up for failure. What one human can successfully complete the full-time jobs of 4 employees within the same 40-hour workweek?

I walked to retrieve my documents from the printer. I remember walking back to my desk thinking, "this is not my life". Working in an abusive environment presented no options for me to succeed. I never experienced someone so hateful and rude. She made comments of how a black woman should not be allowed to drive my type of car. She said that I was lucky to get my bachelor's degree because her (non-black) daughter was experiencing challenges enrolling in school.

I prayed and asked God to teach me how to love my enemies.

I asked God how I could show her the "good" in me. That request was a poor use of my energy. She decided to file a formal reprimand. It was my only negative record I ever received from any employer. The reprimand stated that she could terminate my employment in 30 days without cause or notice.

Listen, some people will never like you. Some people are so jealous or scared of the greatness inside of you that they will do everything in their power to belittle you.

Jealousy and hatred make people do hurtful things. When they can't control you, they try to control how other people perceive you. They attack your character with lies that they created to make others view you as a bad person. Them imagining that you're a bad person allows them to not feel guilty for the way they treat you. It's easier when they are in a higher level of authority over you. They exercise their power in ways that will leave you confused and scratching your head.

Don't try to make sense of "crazy".
Don't try to convince people to treat you with respect.

Just understand that they will never like you, have chosen to perceive you negatively, and it is not up to you to try and make them see the good in you. You let them be jealous and angry. You stop thinking that you are the problem. You are not. When you have done everything you can to be the peacemaker, and work with integrity, they have the problem, not you. It does not matter how kind, respectful, or accommodating you are. Jealousy and hatred despise the light of your spiritual greatness.

Back at work, I continued to pray: Thy kingdom come, Thy will be done. I prayed that the evil wickedness in the atmosphere be arrested by goodness and the power of God's word. My professional mentor warned me of what my racist manager and her partner in human resources could do. She prepared me with my options. She was extremely wise and experienced in corporate politics. Over the next 30 days, I printed my evidentiary emails. I trusted God and refused to live in fear.

My employment was terminated 30 days hence. As I walked out of that building with my box of personal items, I smiled. I knew I was going to be okay. I smiled because my new journey was beginning. I had no idea what was ahead of me. I knew that anything I experienced was going to work in my favor and benefit me along the way. My smile grew, even larger, the moment I realized I no longer had to spend 45+ hours each week being verbally abused, belittled or disrespected.

I was free.

There was a moment of concern where I thought, "how will I pay my bills, car note and mortgage". But then, I reminded myself that I prayed, "God's will be done".

When my thoughts tried to magnify into fear of not having enough money or losing control of paying my bills, I spoke against my thoughts in prayer. Within 14 days, my mortgage was paid. Within 3 weeks, my car note was paid-off in-full. God made a way, like always. Knowing that God's will was for me to be free from that abusive environment gave me an overwhelming peace. God would take care of me.

If they fire you, so what? God is your source and that job is only a resource. When God wants to remove you from an employer or a relationship, God sometimes uses rejection, eviction, or other means to move you. Usually this brings the highest levels of discomfort and growth. It's all part of stretching your faith. The trying of your faith creates patience in you and your confidence in God.

Sometimes there's a fear of rejection when something bad happens. Because of this, worry can consume our thoughts. What if I lose my car? What if I lose my house? What if I don't get another job? What if I don't have enough money for this or that? What if I fail this test? These thoughts tried to consume my day for about 5 months after walking out of that horrible place.

Then, God asked me why I was afraid to also trust with my credit score. Did God not control the banks and my money anyway? Once I realized that my perfect credit score did not determine my worth or my value, I was able to surrender that major piece of control. In faith and belief, I was free from the worry of not being able to pay every bill in full. I knew that my 'faith' in God was the way I would survive.

I had to shift my thoughts from "what if" to "God has it". I changed my perspective from "I can't" to "God can". It was no longer my responsibility to take care of me. It was God's responsibility to take care of my needs. It has not been easy. Nevertheless, I know that my affliction is purposeful for the faith that God is creating within me.

Where is your faith and trust in God?

What area in your life are your thoughts trying to make you worry about things that have yet to occur? Stop worrying and start believing. Stop the contrary thoughts and start speaking, out loud, that God will care for your every need. Change your thinking, within the battlefield of your mind, and fight with the affirming thoughts of good. What does God say about your situation? Source will supply every need. Fear not. God is in control.

God knew this day would come and has already predestined a solution to this challenge. Stretch your faith. God can do more than we (according to faith) can ask or think. We are responsible for activating our faith. God is responsible for being true to every Word. God always provides, always.

# 21

## <u>CHANGE AGENT</u>

You're a natural builder, helper, and change agent. Give you a vision; you will bring it to completion. As a change agent, expect that most people will challenge your progress for improvement. People like the safety of things remaining the same. Know that because you have so many gifts and abilities to improve companies and the lives of people around you, you'll also gain a lot of enemies.

I am praying for your strength to manifest the completed work.

Men, as change agents, are leaders and visionaries. Women, as change agents, are the strength, benefit and energy.

Men, pursue your vision and passion with vigor and fervor. We will support you. We will give our "everything" to manifest your vision. We are the favor to your success. We will love you endlessly and support you tirelessly as the priests of our homes and the love of our lives.

Thank you for your strength. Again, I am praying for your strength to complete the work.

# 22

# <u>MISUNDERSTOOD</u>

At times I found myself in a room full of people but knowing I was different. It wasn't necessarily the way I looked. It wasn't that I spoke differently from other people. I was simply unique. I knew I was different. From the way I thought, to how I carried myself, I felt different.

Listen, beloved. You were wired a certain way and created for great things. Of course you're different. No one else can love like you love. No one else can impact your neighborhood and family, like you can. God knew exactly how to create you: fearfully and wonderfully unique. Your quirks, the way you think, are all for you to complete your unique purpose. No one can do it the way you do. No one can tell them the way you can. It's okay to be exactly who God has created you to be: quirky and uniquely different. Other people are still trying to figure out who they are. Truth of the matter is, they don't like you because they can't understand you. Most of them don't even like themselves.

You're not for them to understand and it's not for you to try and make people understand you. It is your job and role to understand you. Please stop losing sleep over being misunderstood. They will never understand you because you're different.

Your uniqueness is a GIFT.

What I learned in the process of understanding myself is that there are people who are focused on not understanding me, intentionally. Anything I say, they won't catch it and will focus on the smallest, most insignificant way that they can disagree with what I say or do. That's their goal. Those types of people are

everywhere. Beloved, stand firm in your truth and
uniqueness. All great leaders are misunderstood.
You're in good company.

# 23

## <u>INTEGRITY > BEAUTY</u>

No ma'am, sir. I remember folks wanting to know how I "got there" or why I was given access to certain elite offices. Someone had the nerve to say that I flirted my way or that I was fast, simply because I was beautiful. Sorry, not sorry. I was and will always be a woman of integrity.

In spite of my integrity, it was much easier for them to degrade me because of my appearance or become jealous than it was to actually imagine that I worked hard and genuinely valued everyone I have the opportunity to meet. When those that did see my genuine heart began to embrace me, it made the onlookers even more jealous.

You are a person of integrity.

Jealous people attack your reputation by trying to control how other people see you through manipulation. Small minds will listen. Don't give them any thought. You cannot allow other people's perception of you to change your self-esteem.

Continue in integrity. People who love you know that you work hard and keep your legs closed. Don't mind the haters. Their wind will eventually fail.

# 24

## JUST SAY NO

In order to advance in life you must become comfortable with confrontation. If you choose not to speak up for yourself, eventually you'll die defeated and resentful.

For the majority of my life, I applied this scripture to my peers, colleagues, and church family: Romans 12:10, "Be devoted to one another in love. Honor one another above yourselves." I made sure that others had what they needed even if taking care of them was harmful to me. I ensured that other people were happy at the expense of my own happiness. It wasn't until I had nothing to give that I realized I needed to take care of myself. I can't give what I don't have. I cannot live my life allowing everyone else to use me but God.

I was the one responsible for managing my time, my health, and my resources.

I am responsible for my life and my choices.

I had to stop trying to please people and stop making choices that would make other people happy.

The problem with putting other people first is that it teaches them to put you second.

I recognized that the request for my time and resources were requests from *people* and were not assignments from *God*.

I had to go through a period of saying "no" to a lot of requests; for my health, for my well-being.

Stop allowing others to use you.

Stop allowing others to take your resources. Stop giving your time to people who only value you as much as they can use you. "Givers" must set limits because "users" do not.

If you say "no", users always find someone else to do it. Users always find someone else to help them.

Say "No".
Let them ask someone else.

"No" is a complete answer.

# 25

# SILENCE, ≠THE ANSWER

How do you respond to being misunderstood? Remain quiet? Is it pointless to argue? Should you make a scene? Nah, keep quiet to avoid confrontation and be 'liked'. (sarcastically speaking)

Silence does not guarantee protection.

"When you speak, you are afraid your words will not be heard or welcomed. When you are silent you are still afraid. So it is better to speak. Realizing we were never meant to survive". -Audre Lorde

Silence is acceptance.

"Our lives begin to end the day we become silent about things that matter"
~ Dr. Martin Luther King, Jr.

Your silence is keeping you prisoner to the fear of the opinions of others. Stop living in fear of being misunderstood.

Your words have power
Your words are important
Your words are significant

SPEAK and transcend the weight of silence
SPEAK and reverberate strength
SPEAK and resound grace
SPEAK and destroy fear
SPEAK and ascend doubt......SPEAK

They hear "power" when you speak.

# 26

## CONDESCENDING

Condescending people are only speaking to you from their perspective of you; not who you really are. Condescending people speak to you from their own perspective of how they feel about themselves; not who you really are. Ask them, "why are you talking to me like this"? Ask them, "What does that mean"? They will keep talking crazy until you address their behavior. Don't be afraid to question their condescending tone. #Check it. #CheckThem

# 27

## <u>**LIKES**</u>

Approval from the right people can grow your chest beyond giants. Approval from the wrong people can kill your dreams.

Learn to seek God's approval, only. Seek approval within <u>yourself</u>.

To the person that may be enslaved by the opinions of others; the only solution is to change your thinking to who God says you are. Stop exalting "people" and their opinion above your own. They aren't more important than you. Their opinion does not matter more than yours.

You matter. You matter. You matter.

You are important. You owe it to yourself, the wonderful person that God created in infinite likeness, to be strong in God; not in the opinions of other people.

Set your mind on the things that God says about you. You are fearfully and wonderfully made. You have been equipped to handle this season of your life. Nothing is too hard for God. This has to be handled between you and your creator. Your strength to survive this, and other tests like it, is found in the confident security of your self-confident, self-assured, God-self. Yes, you must enhance your God-self = understanding who you are within this created universe.

Magnify what God says about you louder than disbelief.

Magnify it louder than the voice in your head.

Magnify it louder than naysayers, pessimists, or cynics.

Confidence and Security within yourself is the only way to be free from the opinions of others.

# THE

# RELIGION

The hair on their heads wasn't singed, their clothes weren't burned, and they didn't smell of smoke.

Daniel 3:27

# 28

## <u>ANGEL IN HELL</u>

Sometimes we find ourselves in environments that feel like HELL. Behave with confidence and integrity in environments created for your demise. These "hell" places can include: corporate walls, mass incarceration, or religious churches.

You were created to be "light" in darkness. You can survive the environments of Hell. While you're planning your escape, grasp the following lessons:

1. Don't let them use/exhaust your talents. Your skills, talents, and abilities are unto God, not for anyone else; Colossians 3:23. You live your life. Or other people will live your life, for you.

2. Don't lower your weapon just because your enemy smiled. Your enemies won't change. There will always want a fight; Luke 17:1

3. Once the naïve, "Everyone is good", finally met the realistic, "these folks are crazy and don't give a crap about you",

Your mental approach will change to self-actualization, self-priority, and self-love.

The confines of mental bondage will no longer hold you. You will unlock your spirit.

You'll have the opportunity to escape mental HELL (and the fiery furnace) with your wings **still** intact.

# 29

# TELL THEM "NO"

-Freedom from them taking advantage-

Our church had guests coming into town for a conference. Being a servant leader, I volunteered to help assist. The conference ministry leader requested that we be flexible in fulfilling requests that may be outside of the norm. To my surprise, this meant driving to the airport at multiple times within the day, and all hours of the night, to pick up numerous guest speakers, find money to pay for parking, shuttle the speakers around all day, have some of the speakers stay in my home, take them to dinner, cook for them, take them shopping; just to name a few.

After the conference ended, I was compensated with $100. I was beyond shocked. Are you serious? All that

I did (total cost $1,712.53) at their request and I was only given $100. I was hurt. I was angry. It was at that moment that I realized I was allowing people to use me. I remember feeling obligated to help those who asked me to give my money, time, and resources but struggled because my resources were limited. Yes, servant leadership tells us that Jesus did not come to be served, but to serve, Mark 10:25. And the greatest among you will be your servant, Matthew 23:11. Serving others was my lifestyle but this felt wrong.

During this time, I spent more time in devotion and seeking God's plan for my life. God reminded me of the assignments and talents God gave me that I was responsible for, unto God. God said,

"Only do what I tell you to do."

I felt restored and energized. I felt equipped and empowered. I felt ready to be led by God to fulfill *my* purpose in Creation and less obligated to meet the requests of other people.

It was in that moment that I vowed to exercise my right to say "No" more than ever. If it was not a God-given assignment, but a person's request, my answer was "No". Saying "No" began to free me from the obligations or requests of others. Every time I said "No", I felt as if I survived someone else trying to place a responsibility weight on my shoulders. "No" became my freedom. I hear you say, but what if God wanted you to say, "Yes"? Oh, believe me, I took their requests to God before I even replied. God's answer to me was, "tell them No". I began to value my time and energy more than allowing other people to use my gifts and talents for their gain. I stopped being a "people-pleaser." I had weeks of time where I had nothing scheduled. Just because my schedule was available, no longer meant that I should fill it with meeting the requests of others.

People that want to keep you enslaved to their requests would have you think you have to do everything that someone asks you to do, especially in church leadership. Just because someone with a title makes a request of you, does not obligate you to meet the request. You and God are the orchestrators of your life, not folk with church titles, or pastors. You're not required to complete everything that all the leaders with titles request of you and spend no time investing in your personal relationship. Being "yes, men/women" to everyone's requests fail you in fulfilling *your* God-given purpose. I encourage you to exercise your power to say, "No".

Self-evaluate the times or moments when you didn't ask yourself if an opportunity was something Spirit wanted you to do, or if it was something that people requested you do. Build your self-esteem, self-worth, and self-value above the ability for others to use you. Pray that God speaks clearly about what requests or assignments are "God-led" and which requests are not.

You can be free from the obligations of others.

Don't you dare feel bad for not allowing someone to use you.

Don't you dare feel bad for saying, "No".

Don't you dare feel bad for choosing your happiness in spite of how others might view you.

You've made their happiness a priority long enough.

Change has come.

You are now THEE priority.

# 30

## <u>BLOCKED</u>

Everyone does not deserve access to you. Every phone call you receive doesn't need to be answered. Every question does not deserve a response.

Some people are just nosy.
Some people just want access to you for their personal gain.

You control your circle.
You are the creator of your community.
You are not obligated to let leeches in.

# 31

## <u>FORGIVENESS ≠ RECONCILIATION</u>

It also does not give them another chance to make you miserable, disappointed, or steal your peace.

Forgiveness only means that you now see who they are and know how to protect yourself from them.

It does not mean that you trust them again.
It does not mean that we are friends or can be friends.

It does not mean they get a fresh start.
It simply means you release the hurt or anger for what they did and choose to respond to them with love **from a distance**.

Tell them:

"God bless you. You are no longer allowed to occupy this place in my life or my heart."

There is no room for them in your life.

Sorry, No Vacancy.

# 32

## <u>ESCAPE THE CAVE<br>OF RELIGION</u>

You can't see the picture when you are inside the
frame.

You can't experience the world if you are still inside
the cave.

They won't be happy for you.

They are blind, in the cave, themselves.

They can't see that there is a way out.

The pursuit of truth, of a higher better life, of
freedom, is hidden while you are in the cave with
them.

Once you pursue truth, chase knowledge, hunt for
liberty, you can escape.

Get out. Be free.

Don't expect them to celebrate the fact that you are free; that you escaped. You broke chains of religious mental bondage.

You were bound in that cave long enough.
Release your spirit to walk in the fullness and newness of complete freedom.

You are no longer "religion".
You are "limitless liberty".

#Plato's Allegory of The Cave  #2Kings7:3

# I Get Out

Song Lyrics by Lauryn Hill

"Psychological locks

Repressing true expression

Cementing this repression

Promoting mass deception

So that no one can be healed

I don't respect your system

I won't protect your system

When you talk I don't listen

Oh, let my Father's will be done

And just get out

Oh, just get out of all this bondage

Just get out

Oh, you can't hold me in these chains

Just get out" Oh, you can't hold me in chains

Just get out

All these traditions killin' freedom

Knowin' my condition

Is the reason I must change

I've just accepted what you said

Keepin' me among the dead

The only way to know

Is to walk then learn and grow

But faith is not your speed

Oh, you've had everyone believed

That you're the sole authority

Just follow the majority

Afraid to face reality

The system is a joke

Oh, you'd be smart to save your soul

Oh, when escape is mind control

You spent your life in sacrifice

To a system for the dead

Oh, are you sure...

Where is the passion in this living

Are you sure it's God you servin'

Obligated to a system

Getting less then you're deserving

Who made up these schools, I say

Who made up these rules, I say

Animal conditioning

Oh, just to keep us as a slave


"I Get Out" lyrics written by: Lauryn Hill

**Thank you for being magic...**

# 33

# THEY'RE FOUL & YOU'RE MEMORABLE MAGIC

You create for them to grow their success. They promise to return "grand appreciation". When they finally reached success, they "forgot" about you. Why is it that people refuse to say "thank you" publicly (or privately)? Oh, they are okay with keeping you a secret but never acknowledging your work or that you were the largest (98%) benefit to their success?

Now, hurt ensues because you trusted them to reciprocate the love/time/resources you invested and they refuse to say "thank you".

Beloved, no. They didn't forget about you. They ignored you, intentionally. Their plans to take credit for your work will fail if they acknowledge your efforts.

They talk about you negatively behind your back. So, they can't thank you or acknowledge you in public. That's why they say they "forgot". They want to take your hard work and put their name on it. God is not unjust. God will reward you for helping people even if they *say* they "forgot". Heb 6:10

No problem. Let them say that they "forgot" to acknowledge you. Eventually, when your shine is blinding, they'll be telling everyone how connected you all are and riding your coattails. Um, No. (Keep that same energy) #

Celebrate me now, not after my shine is blinding you and your congregation. The way people mistreat those that have invested in them still blows my mind and makes me confused. Just treat people right. It is that easy.

The right people will celebrate your success.
The right people will support your dreams.
The right people will remember you.
The right people will say "thank you" without being prompted.
The right people will show you support, without you looking for it.

Remember*
You're unforgettable, baby. You're magic.

Relax,

Let God Justify You.

# CONCLUSION

Everyone can't go with you. God allows relationships to end when they no longer benefit your personal growth. God also allows us to journey through some experiences between you and the universe alone, just to reveal how powerful you are. Look at how much you have survived!

~

We never understand the lens of another person until we comprehend where their experience has taken them before. So, allow your experience to take you places you've never been and embrace new understandings.

~

To the single parent, the victor after divorce, the ambitious man, the modern woman, the person who has no other choice but to trust God with their heart and for their strength: I commend you for not quitting.

You are my hero, my muse, my ally along this journey.

May God continue to strengthen you to do great things by the works of your hand.

~

This work is the 2nd of its series in hopes that the transparency of our hearts will strengthen each other as we unapologetically journey from Venom to Victory. More books come...

# BIOGRAPHY

Dr. Elle Moore is a motivational speaker, Certified pre-marital counselor, choreographer of worship in arts, and

Co-founder of Vessels of Virtue: a women's holistic ministry that provides practical biblical solutions for women ages 25-40.

As a Doctor of Education in Behavioral Science and Leadership, she holds a Master's Degree in Pastoral Counseling, Bachelor's Degree in Business Management, and various credentials in Executive Leadership in Management.

As an avid volunteer, Dr. Elle Moore is the recipient of more than 29 awards in recognition for her leadership excellence in service to numerous communities including:

* NCSSE, the National Council for Spirit Safety and Education certificate in recognition of excellence in principles and ethics as a mentor and coach for girls ages 9-14,
* Teaching Assistant to autistic primary & elementary students
* City Council's recognition for providing more than 3,000 hours of transformative community service, breaking down social barriers, inspiring citizens to civic action, developing leaders for the common good, improving and promoting national service, and
* Governor Bob Taft's recognition for outstanding dedication of service in literacy and scholastic development of inner city youth.

Her ministry focuses on:
* discipleship and maximizing human capital,
* empowering God's people to live victoriously according to kingdom principles, advancing

individuals forward in fulfilling their God given purpose, and

★ exhorting believers to use their spiritual gifts to serve effectively.

As a transformative servant leader, Dr. Elle Moore continues to seek ways to enhance the individual truth within each person she encounters.

Dr. Elle Moore's desire is that people walk in their purpose for kingdom living according to their established principles. Her heartfelt goal is to teach practical truths that are relevant to her listeners and through relationship building, promote emotional intelligence.

Her sincere prayer is that all of God's people grow in relationship with their creator, partner with the leaders of their organizations, and positively impact their communities

Dr. Elle is the owner of 'Evolve Counseling & Consulting' and 'BlkPen Publishing Company'.

She enjoys: tacos, the charismatic comedy from her nieces and nephews, and being a Plant Mom to: Crayola, Davi, Giuseppe, Odetta, Otto and Trixie (Beatrice).

## Contact Dr. Elle Moore for:

★ Counseling Services

★ Marriage & Couples Counseling

(LGBTQIA+, Non-monogamous, All Trans, Poly, Full-Spectrum, are Welcomed and Affirmed)

★ Speaking Engagements

★ Author Services, Editing, Formatting+ Graphics

 @EvolveCounselingllc    Text (360) EVOLVE-5

 @BlkPenPublishing    Text (559) 8-BlkPen

 www.DrEllle.com

Printed in Great Britain
by Amazon

75619874R00083